# Fast Track Savings

T.S. AVINI

Fast Track Savings

Cut Expenses and Boost Your Emergency Fund Quickly

by T.S. AVINI

# Table of Contents

# Chapter 1: Introduction: The Importance of Quick Savings

In today's fast-paced world, where financial stability can sometimes seem as elusive as a fleeting breeze, the importance of having a robust emergency fund cannot be overstated.

An emergency fund acts as a financial cushion, providing peace of mind and security, enabling you to navigate the unpredictable tides of life with greater confidence. From unexpected medical expenses to sudden job losses or urgent car repairs, an emergency fund can spell the difference between a minor bump in the road and a catastrophic financial derailment.

But why the urgency in building this fund quickly, you may ask? The answer lies in the unpredictable nature of emergencies themselves.

Life rarely offers a convenient schedule for things to go awry. As such, the need for a quick savings strategy, particularly in establishing or boosting your emergency fund, becomes not just a financial best practice but a crucial move toward safeguarding your future.

I've seen this happen before: In this book, "Fast Track Savings: Cut Expenses and Boost Your Emergency Fund Quickly," we aim to arm you with practical tools and insight to rapidly build your financial safety net.

This chapter seeks to lay the foundation by exploring why saving quickly is imperative and how speed can be infused into the art of saving without compromising your essential lifestyle.

Financial Resilience: The Backbone of Quick Savings

Building savings quickly is not merely a response to immediate needs; it's an exercise in cultivating financial resilience. When you have funds readily available to handle emergencies—big or small—you protect yourself from spiraling into debt.

Picture this: a sudden plumbing issue at home requires urgent attention, and with an emergency fund, you can address it directly. Without one, the same issue might mean relying on credit, accruing interest, and eventually paying far more than the actual repair.

It's worth noting that Moreover, having an emergency fund empowers you to make choices.

With financial flexibility, you are less likely to remain trapped in undesirable situations—consider an unbearable job or living situation. The availability of quick savings offers options, making transitions smoother and less stressful.

The Psychology of Saving Fast

Beyond the practicalities of money management, quick savings requires the right mindset.

It's about commitment, the willingness to prioritize future security over immediate gratification, and perhaps most importantly, the cultivation of disciplined financial habits.

Interestingly enough, Psychologically, the act of saving aggressively can create a positive feedback loop, where the satisfaction of watching your savings grow motivates further disciplined behavior.

When you see progress in real time, you're encouraged to continue on this path of financial virtue, redefining your relationship with money from that of an obstacle to a tool for achieving stability and freedom.

Identifying Priorities to Catalyze Savings

Understanding where to start in cutting expenses can be daunting without clarity on what's essential versus optional in your expenditure list. Quick savings necessitates an honest analysis of your spending habits.

Start with necessities—housing, utilities, groceries—and set aside reasonable amounts for these. Identify areas that can be immediately trimmed: subscriptions you rarely use, brand preferences that offer cheaper alternatives without sacrificing quality, or dining habits that could be adjusted without significant lifestyle changes.

I've seen this happen before: Moreover, adopting a minimalist approach to material possessions can result in notable savings.

Consider decluttering your space and selling unused items. Often, less truly is more—a philosophy that translates into fewer purchases, reduced maintenance costs, and a more significant reserve for your emergency fund.

Strategies for Speedy Savings Growth

To expand your emergency fund rapidly, maximize any opportunity for financial inflow.

This could be through side hustles, which utilize skills or hobbies that generate income when your primary job doesn't. From freelance work to online tutoring, or selling handmade crafts, the gig economy offers numerous platforms to make extra cash.

At first glance, Additionally, reroute any unexpected windfalls—bonuses, tax refunds, gifts—from spending and directly into your savings pool.

This practice ensures that these additional funds contribute tangibly to security rather than being absorbed into everyday expenses.

The Role of Technology in Quick Savings

Harness technology to your advantage in this quest for swift savings.

Numerous budgeting apps now help track expenses in real-time, offering insights into spending habits and identifying potential areas for savings. Automation is another strategic tool; set up automatic transfers to your emergency fund from your paycheck, creating a "pay yourself first" system that prioritizes savings over unessential expenses.

Interestingly enough, Tools like high-yield savings accounts or money market accounts can also enhance the efficiency of your savings growth, offering better returns on your deposits than a standard savings account would.

Conclusion: The Path Forward

This chapter merely scratches the surface of the strategies and techniques awaiting exploration throughout this book.

The need for quick savings transcends mere financial strategy; it's about creating a safety net through disciplined practice and thoughtful choices. As you embark on this journey, view each step as an investment in stability and peace, paving the way for reduced stress and greater enjoyment of life's inevitable highs and lows.

It's worth noting that Embarking on a fast-track savings plan requires dedication and a bit of sacrifice, but the payoff—a secure future and the freedom to act when life throws curveballs—is unparalleled.

With the tools within these pages, you will be well on your way to boosting your emergency fund quickly and efficiently. Welcome to a pathway towards financial confidence and independence!.

routinely executed action. Additionally, examine your tax returns to ensure you're maximizing deductions and credits, often spearheading unexpected increases in available income.

Conclusion: Building a Foundation for Success

I've seen this happen before: Assessing your financial landscape is neither a quick task nor a one-time event.

It's an evolving process as your income grows, expenses change, and unexpected challenges occur. The goal is not to achieve financial perfection but to develop a comprehensive understanding that supports informed, effective decision-making.

Achieve this foundational understanding, and you're well-equipped to take the next steps in cutting expenses and bolstering your emergency fund—one smart decision at a time. The more you know about your financial position, the more control you have over your future.

Each insight you gain is a step toward financial resilience and peace of mind. By thoroughly understanding your financial landscape, you lay the groundwork for financial success and long-term stability.

# Chapter 3: Setting Realistic Savings Goals

Establishing realistic savings goals is akin to charting the course for a successful financial journey. It provides direction, motivation, and a tangible destination toward which to work.

Many people set goals but often find themselves adrift due to unattainable expectations. This chapter will guide you through creating practical savings goals that are both challenging and achievable, empowering you to make significant strides toward financial security.

**Understanding Your Why**

Before delving into the mechanics of setting savings goals, it's imperative to understand the "why" behind your aspiration to save.

What motivates you to build a safety net? Is it the peace of mind knowing that you're prepared for emergencies, the desire to purchase a home, or perhaps planning a future getaway? Having a clear motivation fuels commitment and perseverance. Write down your reasons, keeping them visible as a constant reminder of your purpose.

**Assessing Your Financial Landscape**

Begin by taking an inventory of your current financial situation.

This involves understanding your income, expenses, and any existing savings. Create a comprehensive budget, detailing all sources of income and categorizing expenses into fixed (rent, utilities, insurance) and variable (groceries, entertainment, dining out).

It's worth noting that Analyzing your financial landscape allows you to identify areas where you can cut back and allocate more towards savings.

A clear understanding of your financial inflows and outflows establishes a solid foundation for setting goals that are both ambitious and achievable.

**Defining SMART Goals**

The SMART criteria—Specific, Measurable, Achievable, Relevant, and Time-bound—serves as a blueprint for setting effective savings goals. Let's break down how to apply these principles:

I've seen this happen before: - **Specific**: Your savings goals should be clearly defined. Instead of a vague "save more money," specify the exact amount or percentage of income you want to save.

For instance, "Save $500 per month" or "Increase emergency fund to $5,000. ".

- **Measurable**: Goals need to be quantifiable so you can track your progress.

Measurable goals allow you to celebrate small victories along the way and provide a marker against which to measure your progress.

- **Achievable**: While it's important to challenge yourself, your goals must also be attainable. Consider your current financial obligations and lifestyle.

Setting a goal to save half your income may not be feasible if you're living paycheck-to-paycheck. Start with smaller, achievable goals and gradually increase them as your financial situation improves.

Let’s not forget, - **Relevant**: Your savings goals should align with your broader financial objectives and personal values.

Consider whether your goals contribute to your long-term plans, such as buying a home, retirement, or education.

- **Time-bound**: Assign a deadline to each goal to instill a sense of urgency and motivation.

"Save $1,000 in three months" provides a clear timeframe, prompting consistent action and accountability.

**Prioritizing Your Goals**

I’ve seen this happen before: Once you have a list of SMART goals, it's time to prioritize.

Not all goals carry the same weight, and some may require immediate attention. Emergency savings, for instance, should take precedence over non-essential purchases, given its role in cushioning unforeseen financial shocks.

List your goals in order of importance and urgency.

Often, it's beneficial to focus on one goal at a time or balance one primary goal with secondary goals that require less immediate attention. Reassess your list periodically, as priorities can shift over time due to changes in lifestyle or financial circumstances.

**Creating a Savings Plan**

At first glance, With your goals clearly defined and prioritized, the next step is creating a structured savings plan.

Consider the different methods for automating your savings:.

1.

**Direct Deposit Allocations**: Arrange with your employer to deposit a portion of your paycheck directly into a savings account. This "pay yourself first" strategy ensures consistent saving before the money hits your spending account.

2.

**Automatic Transfers**: Set up automatic monthly transfers from your checking to your savings account. This method, like direct deposit, helps enforce discipline and removes the temptation to spend.

Believe it or not, 3.

**Round-Up Savings Apps**: Numerous financial apps can help increase your savings by rounding up purchases to the nearest dollar and saving the difference.

Implementing a plan requires commitment and consistency.

Continue to monitor your progress, adjusting your budget as necessary to stay on track with your savings goals. Keep in mind that any plan should remain flexible, allowing for life's inevitable surprises.

**Celebrating Milestones**

As strange as it sounds, Achieving a savings milestone, no matter how small, is worthy of celebration.

Recognizing these accomplishments boosts morale and encourages ongoing effort. Treat yourself in a way that doesn't derail your financial progress—perhaps a nice meal or a small purchase you've had your eye on.

Remember, the process of saving is a marathon, not a sprint.

Consistent effort over time yields substantial results. Maintaining a positive outlook and rewarding yourself for reaching interim goals will sustain motivation and prevent burnout.

**Dealing with Setbacks**

To be honest, Every financial journey encounters setbacks.

Whether it's an unexpected expense or a temporary income reduction, such events can impede progress. It's crucial to maintain a resilient mindset, viewing setbacks as learning opportunities rather than failures.

In instances of a financial hiccup, reassess your plan, adapt your goals if necessary, and recalibrate your budget.

Lean on the support of financial literacy resources or consult a financial advisor for tailored guidance if necessary.

**Adapting and Evolving**

Believe it or not, Your savings strategy should evolve alongside changes in your life.

Major life events like a new job, marriage, parenthood, or purchasing a home can significantly impact your financial situation. Revisit your goals periodically, ensuring they remain relevant and aligned with your current priorities and resources.

In conclusion, setting realistic savings goals empowers you to take charge of your financial future. By understanding your motivations, assessing your financial landscape, and implementing the SMART framework, you create a robust path toward achieving your objectives.

Remember, this journey is personal, and progress is a testament to your discipline, determination, and dedication to securing your financial well-being. Let each goal reached be a stepping stone to greater financial freedom and security.

# Chapter 4: The Fast Track Mindset: Psychology of Saving

For many, the concept of saving money is akin to dieting. It involves restraint, discipline, and occasionally a sense of deprivation.

However, just as a successful diet is less about total abstinence and more about a balanced approach to eating, successful saving hinges on cultivating the right mindset. The fast track to savings isn't a mere series of monetary transactions; it's a psychological journey that requires understanding, patience, and perspective. In this chapter, we explore how adopting a fast track mindset can transform how you perceive and manage your finances, ultimately enabling you to accelerate your savings goals.

Understanding Your Money Mindset

At first glance, Before diving into practical strategies, it's crucial to understand your current relationship with money. Everyone has a unique money mindset shaped by past experiences, family upbringing, and societal influences.

To develop a fast track saving mindset, start with introspection. Ask yourself:.

- How do you perceive money? Is it a source of stress or opportunity?

Believe it or not, - What emotional triggers cause you to spend impulsively?

- How did your family handle money, and how does that influence your habits today?

By identifying the answers to these questions, you gain insight into the deep-seated beliefs that guide your financial decisions.

Only by understanding your starting point can you begin to reshape your approach to saving.

Reframing Saving as Positive

Many people view saving as a loss—money taken away from today's pleasures.

This negative framing can hinder motivation and make it difficult to stay committed to saving. The key to changing this perception is to reframe saving in a positive light.

I've seen this happen before: Consider saving not as renunciation but as empowerment. Each dollar saved is a step toward future security, a means of accessing opportunities, and a safeguard against life's uncertainties.

Visualize this process not as deprivation but as a method for improving your overall well-being. When saving becomes synonymous with empowerment, staying the course feels less burdensome.

Setting Clear and Compelling Goals

Goals are the roadmap to effective saving. Without them, financial planning can feel aimless and overwhelming.

Align your savings with clear, compelling goals to give purpose and direction to your efforts. Instead of vague objectives like "save more money," identify specific targets such as building a $5,000 emergency fund within a year or setting aside $200 each month for a family vacation.

Believe it or not, Make these goals visible in your daily life.

Write them down, create vision boards, or set reminders on your phone. The constant awareness of your goals helps shape your daily choices and reinforces the importance of your saving efforts.

The Power of Habit Formation

Adopting the fast track saving mindset involves creating new habits and routines that support your financial goals.

According to Charles Duhigg, author of *The Power of Habit*, habits follow a loop: cue, routine, reward. Establishing saving as a habit means identifying cues that trigger saving behaviors, defining routines that make saving automatic, and ensuring rewards reinforce these behaviors.

It's worth noting that A practical strategy is to set up automated transfers from your checking to savings accounts on payday.

The cue is receiving your paycheck, the routine is the automated transfer, and the reward is watching your savings grow with minimal effort. By automating this process, the decision to save is no longer a recurring struggle; it becomes a part of your financial routine.

Managing Temptation: Mindful Spending

A fast track mindset isn't solely about what you save; it's also about how you spend. Mindful spending involves being acutely aware of your financial choices, distinguishing needs from wants, and making informed decisions.

Implementing a 24-hour rule for non-essential purchases is an effective method to curb impulse buying. If you see an item you want that's not on your necessity list, wait a full day before making the purchase. This delay often reduces the impulse and allows you to evaluate the significance of the purchase rationally.

In real life, Another technique is to categorize expenses into 'joyful' and 'mindless' spending. Joyful spending aligns with values and enhances quality of life—such as spending on a hobby or dining with friends.

Mindless spending, by contrast, is often an automatic response to stress, boredom, or peer pressure. Once identified, cut back on mindless expenditures to free up more room in your budget for saving without sacrificing contentment.

Overcoming Setbacks with Resilience

Financial challenges and setbacks are inevitable, but how you respond to them is what defines success. Cultivating resilience is an integral part of the fast track mindset.

Approach setbacks as learning opportunities rather than failures. Ask yourself:.

- What circumstances led to this setback?

- How can I prevent similar situations in the future?

- What action can I take to get back on track quickly?

By developing a resilient attitude, you empower yourself to navigate through financial hiccups with determination and poise, keeping your long-term goals firmly in sight.

Celebrating Milestones and Keeping Motivation High

Persisting in your saving journey requires regular motivation. Recognize and celebrate milestones, regardless of size.

Small achievements add up over time and provide tangible evidence of progress. Celebrate by finding non-financial rewards, such as a day to relax or a planned activity you enjoy.

Additionally, keep your motivation high by educating yourself continuously about personal finance.

The more knowledgeable you become, the more confident you will feel in managing your money, making informed decisions, and achieving your goals.

Embracing the Community of Savers

Finally, engaging with a community of like-minded individuals can immensely bolster your saving efforts.

Whether through online forums, social media groups, or local workshops, sharing experiences and strategies can introduce fresh perspectives and reinforce your commitment. Communicating with others about money goals and challenges lessens the isolation people often feel on financial journeys and offers a support network that empathizes with your aspirations.

Conclusion

The fast track mindset is about transforming your relationship with money, cultivating habits that prioritize savings, and maintaining an unwavering focus on your financial objectives. It's about shifting perception, setting deliberate goals, and embracing a lifestyle of proactive financial management.

By adopting this mindset, you not only accelerate your path to savings but also create a foundation for enduring financial security. As you proceed, remember that the journey is just as significant as the destination. Stay committed, remain flexible, and let your financial mindset drive you toward the abundant future you envision.

# Chapter 5: Budgeting: The Foundation of Financial Health

In the realm of personal finance, budgeting plays a role akin to that of a solid foundation when constructing a house; without it, the entire structure is at risk of collapse.

If you aim to cut expenses and boost your emergency fund quickly, understanding and implementing a well-thought-out budget is paramount. This chapter will guide you through the practical steps of creating and maintaining a robust budget, turning financial stability from a distant goal into an achievable reality.

**Understanding the Importance of Budgeting**

As strange as it sounds, Before diving into the mechanics of budgeting, it's crucial to grasp why budgeting is indispensable for financial health. A budget provides clarity.

It transforms abstract numbers into a clear financial roadmap, highlighting where your money comes from and where it goes. More importantly, it unveils opportunities for savings – funds that can be redirected into an emergency fund or other financial goals.

**Step One: Assess Your Income**

The first step in creating a budget is to determine your total income after taxes. This income could be from various sources such as your salary, freelance work, investments, or side gigs.

Knowing your exact income is critical because it sets the parameters within which you must work. Avoid the common mistake of overestimating this figure, as it can lead to unrealistic budgeting and potential overspending.

**Step Two: Track Your Expenses**

Before you can cut expenses, you need a comprehensive understanding of your existing spending habits. Track all your expenditures meticulously for a month.

This includes fixed costs like rent or mortgage payments, utilities, insurance, and minimum debt payments, as well as variable expenses such as groceries, dining out, entertainment, and transport. Use technology to your advantage by leveraging budget tracking apps that can automatically categorize and analyze expenses, giving you detailed insights with minimal effort.

**Step Three: Categorize and Analyze Your Spending**

To be honest, Once you have a record of your spending, categorize these expenses into fixed and variable groups. Fixed expenses are non-negotiable and relatively consistent each month.

In contrast, variable expenses offer opportunities for adjustment. Analyzing these categories not only reveals your spending patterns but also helps you identify areas where you can cut back. For instance, you might discover that impromptu dining or spontaneous purchases consume a significant portion of your budget.

**Step Four: Set Financial Goals**

Having a budget is meaningless without clear objectives. Decide what financial health looks like for you. Perhaps it's a three-month emergency fund or even a more ambitious six-month reserve.

Set specific, measurable financial goals, and ensure they are attainable within a realistic timeframe. Assign these goals as line items in your budget, treating savings as an essential expense rather than an afterthought. This mindset shift is critical for prioritizing your financial wellbeing.

**Step Five: Create Your Budget Plan**

With a thorough understanding of your income, expenses, and financial goals, you can now craft a detailed budget plan. Subtract your total monthly expenses from your income.

Ideally, there should be a surplus - this is the portion of your income that can be routed into savings and your emergency fund. If there's a deficit, you'll need to make adjustments, particularly in variable expenses, to balance your budget.

Adopt a budgeting method that suits your lifestyle and financial situation.

The 50/30/20 rule is a popular method where 50% of your income goes to necessities, 30% to wants, and 20% to savings. Alternatively, you might prefer a zero-based budget, which allocates every dollar to a specific purpose, ensuring income minus expenses is zero.

**Step Six: Implement and Adjust**

Having crafted your budget, the next step is implementation.

This requires discipline and may involve lifestyle changes. Encourage accountability by sharing your budget goals with a trusted friend or family member or by joining community groups focused on financial wellness.

Monitor your budget regularly, ideally monthly, and adjust as necessary.

Life circumstances can change, and your budget should be flexible enough to adapt. The key is not to view a budget as restrictive but as a tool that empowers you to make intentional choices about your spending.

**Step Seven: Embrace Frugality and Creativity**

To cut expenses effectively, adopt a mindset of frugality and creativity. This doesn't mean living a life of deprivation, but rather being resourceful and finding cost-effective ways to meet your needs.

For example, meal planning and cooking at home can significantly reduce food expenses. Explore free or low-cost entertainment options in your community, negotiate bills, or perhaps barter services with friends and neighbors.

**Conclusion: Mastering Budgeting for Financial Health**

Let's not forget, Budgeting is not a one-time event but a continuous journey requiring dedication and willingness to adjust. Mastering budgeting will not only help you cut unnecessary expenses and bolster your emergency fund but also provide a solid foundation for long-term financial health.

Remember, it's not about how much you earn but how wisely you manage what you have. With a robust budget, the financial peace of mind you've been seeking is well within your reach.

# Chapter 6: Cutting Unnecessary Expenses: Identify and Eliminate

In the journey towards financial wellness, the phrase "cutting expenses" often sounds daunting, as if requiring a drastic change in lifestyle or forgoing pleasures that enrich your life. However, the process is more about recognizing and eliminating unnecessary expenditures rather than depriving yourself.

The key is to spend wisely and ensure that each dollar serves a significant purpose, ideally contributing to your broader financial goals, such as building an emergency fund. This chapter will guide you through a strategic approach to identifying and eliminating unnecessary expenses, ensuring that your savings journey stays on the fast track.

Conduct a Comprehensive Expense Audit

I've seen this happen before: The first step in addressing unnecessary expenses is a no-nonsense audit of your current spending habits.

This means taking an unflinching look at where your money goes on a monthly, or even weekly, basis. Remember, you can't fix what you aren't willing to confront.

1.

**Gather Documentation**: Start by gathering bank statements, credit card bills, and any receipts you've accumulated. The past three months serve as a good sample size to identify spending patterns.

2.

**Categorize Your Spending**: Break down your spending into categories such as groceries, dining out, utilities, subscriptions, entertainment, and transportation. Categorization helps in understanding which areas consume the largest portion of your income.

3.

**Analyze Your Findings**: Look for patterns. Are there categories where spending spikes unexpectedly? Are these expenditures consistent with your priorities and values? Recognize areas where you might be overspending due to habit rather than necessity.

Identify the Culprits

Once your spending is laid bare, it's time to pinpoint unnecessary expenses—those often hidden or habitual expenditures eating away at your budget without adding value to your life.

I've seen this happen before: 1. **Subscriptions and Memberships**: This is often a goldmine for unnecessary spending.

Audit all subscriptions—magazines, apps, streaming services, gym memberships, club fees—that you're barely using. Determine which are superfluous, and cancel them. Websites and apps like Truebill or Bobby can help keep track of such recurring charges.

2. **Eating Out vs.

Dining In**: Dining out frequently is a common budget buster. If you find a significant portion of your funds going towards restaurant meals or take-out, consider reducing the frequency. Cooking at home, even a few additional times a week, is both economical and often healthier.

3. **Retail Therapy and Impulse Purchases**: Unnecessary online shopping and impulsive buys at physical stores are tempting yet detrimental.

Implement a waiting period, such as 48 hours, before purchasing non-essentials. Often, the desire will pass, saving you money.

Let's not forget, 4.

**Utilities and Household Services**: Reevaluate your utility expenses. Are you overpaying for internet services you don't fully utilize? Could you reduce energy bills by being more conscious of your consumption? Simple changes, like turning off lights, unplugging electronics, and using energy-efficient appliances, can lead to substantial savings.

5.

**Transportation Options**: Consider how you can cut back on transportation costs. Could you use public transport more often, bike, or carpool to reduce gas and parking fees? Additionally, verify that your car insurance is competitive—sometimes bundling policies or adjusting your coverage can result in savings.

Embrace Budgeting Tools and Techniques

I've seen this happen before: One potent method to survey and subsequently cut unnecessary expenses is the use of budgeting tools.

Whether you prefer a digital app or an old-school spreadsheet, the important factor is consistency and awareness.

1.

**Set a Realistic Budget**: With knowledge of your spending comes the ability to craft a realistic budget. Allocate funds based on necessary expenses, savings goals, and some discretionary spending that aligns with your values.

2.

**Zero-Based Budgeting**: This method involves telling every dollar where to go, ensuring that income minus outgoings equals zero. By assigning each dollar, you diminish the chance of overspending in certain areas.

As strange as it sounds, 3.

**Utilize Budgeting Software**: Apps like Mint, YNAB (You Need A Budget), or personal capital not only aid in tracking expenses but also offer insights into spending habits and areas for cutbacks.

4. **Review Regularly**: A budget isn't a set-and-forget tool.

Make a habit of reviewing your budget monthly and adjusting categories as needed. The goal is to ensure optimized spending that supports your financial goals and lifestyle changes.

Foster a Mindful Spending Mindset

Believe it or not, Long-term success in cutting unnecessary expenses comes from developing a mindset geared towards mindful spending.

This involves being intentional with your purchases and differentiating between needs and wants.

1.

**Pause and Reflect**: Before making purchases, especially larger ones, ask yourself if this aligns with your financial goals. Is it a need or a want? Could satisfaction come from an alternative, less costly solution?.

2. **Incorporate Value-Based Spending**: Focus on what truly brings you joy and fulfillment.

Sometimes, we spend on things because we feel we should, due to societal pressure. Reorient spending towards matters that align with your core values.

Interestingly enough, 3. **Reward System**: Set goals and implement a reward system.

As you see progress, treat yourself modestly. Rewarding yourself maintains motivation, as long as it doesn't derail your financial trajectory.

Conclusion

Through identification and elimination, cutting unnecessary expenses positions you closer to your savings milestones, particularly building a robust emergency fund. This chapter's insights and strategies transform how you perceive and practice spending—cutting costs where it counts while maintaining a fulfilling lifestyle.

The discipline you cultivate in these early steps fosters a healthier, more sustainable financial future. So, arm yourself with determination, patience, and the strategies in this chapter, and embark on a transformative journey toward financial savvy and independence.

# Chapter 7: Smart Shopping: Strategies for Everyday Savings

In an era where consumerism encroaches upon every aspect of life, mastering the art of smart shopping can transform your financial landscape.

By adopting savvy strategies, you can significantly slash your expenses and funnel those savings into your emergency fund, fast-tracking your journey to financial security. This chapter unfolds practical approaches to help you become a conscious consumer, cutting costs without compromising on your needs and sometimes even your wants.

Understand Your Needs versus Wants

Before heading to the store or browsing online, clarify the distinction between needs and wants.

Needs are essentials—items you require for basic living, such as groceries, household supplies, and clothing basics. Wants, on the other hand, are items you desire but can live without, like that extra pair of designer shoes or an upgraded electronic gadget.

To get started, list the items you intend to buy and categorize them.

Scrutinize your list and ask yourself, "Do I need this, or do I want it?" This simple exercise of mindfulness can dramatically change your shopping behavior, helping you to stay focused and avoid the pitfalls of impulsive buying.

Make a Shopping List and Stick to It

Once you've sorted your needs from your wants, make a comprehensive shopping list. Whether it's for groceries or clothing, a list guides your shopping trip, reducing the likelihood of picking up unnecessary items.

Be disciplined about sticking to your list unless you find a more economically viable substitute for something on it or spot a significant bargain on an essential. The key is to be flexible but not frivolous.

Moreover, maintain your list across multiple shopping trips by noting items as they are consumed.

This way, you create consistency in purchasing, avoiding unnecessary multiple trips which often lead to additional, unplanned purchases.

Use Coupons and Discounts Wisely

In real life, Coupons and discounts can be your best allies when shopping smart.

With the rise of digital coupons and discount codes, you don't have to sift through newspapers to find deals. Numerous apps and websites consolidate these offers, making it easier to access savings on the go.

However, a golden rule is to avoid purchasing an item merely because you have a coupon. Unnecessary purchases, even at a discounted price, add up quickly.

Instead, look for coupons on items you need. Combine coupons and store discounts when possible to maximize your savings.

Plan Your Shopping Around Sales Cycles

As strange as it sounds, Retailers operate on sales cycles—seasonal and clearance sales are predictable and ripe for smart savings.

For instance, winter clothes are often discounted in mid-winter and even more during post-season clearance. Plan your major purchases around these cycles to save substantially.

Having said that, it's important to approach sales with caution.

A sale is only a saving if it fits into your needs and budget. Purchasing an item just because it's on sale can derail your savings goals.

Compare Prices

As strange as it sounds, The internet is a powerful tool for price comparison, providing you with information at your fingertips.

Before making a purchase, especially for higher-priced goods, take the time to compare prices from different retailers. Websites and apps like PriceGrabber, Shopzilla, and even Google Shopping can assist you in ensuring you are getting the best deal available.

Price comparison is not limited to physical products.

For subscription services or recurring purchases, be it your mobile plan or insurance, regularly review and compare options to ensure you continue to receive the best value for money.

Buy in Bulk Sensibly

Buying in bulk can yield significant savings, particularly for non-perishable items or goods with a long shelf life like toiletries, cleaning supplies, or canned goods.

Membership-based warehouse clubs often offer bulk deals, which can reduce the per-unit cost of items significantly.

However, bulk buying requires careful planning.

Stockpiling items you will not use before they expire is counter-productive and leads to unnecessary waste, both financial and environmental. Assess your storage capacity and household consumption rate before stocking up, and ensure that you're buying items that you will use in a reasonable timeframe.

Use Cash-Back and Reward Programs

Believe it or not, Many retailers offer reward programs designed to provide cash-back, store credit, or points for use towards future purchases.

Leveraging these programs can lead to incremental savings over time. Credit cards with cash-back features on certain categories like groceries or gas are also worth considering; however, this strategy is only beneficial if you consistently pay your balance in full each month to avoid interest charges.

Practice the 24-Hour Rule

Impulse buying often leads to regret and overspending. Implementing a 24-hour rule can mitigate this risk.

When you're tempted by a non-essential purchase, give yourself a day to think it over. More often than not, the passage of time shifts your perspective, and the item might lose its appeal, allowing you to save both money and unnecessary clutter.

Embrace Second-Hand Shopping

The stigma surrounding second-hand items is fading, giving way to a more sustainable and cost-effective shopping approach.

Thrift stores, online marketplaces, and garage sales offer vast opportunities to purchase quality items at a fraction of the cost new. This approach is especially beneficial for clothing, furniture, and electronics, where the depreciation rate of new items is steep.

Avoid Grocery Shopping on an Empty Stomach

It's worth noting that A simple yet impactful strategy: never grocery shop on an empty stomach.

Hunger can impair your judgment and lead to impulse purchases of unnecessary and often unhealthy items. Make it a habit to plan your grocery shopping after a meal, ensuring you stick more closely to your list and your budget.

Conclusion

Smart shopping is a blend of disciplined strategies and mindful habits. By implementing these practical tips, you embark on a path toward efficient spending, freeing up resources that can contribute significantly to your emergency fund.

Remember, every dollar saved is a dollar earned toward a more secure financial future. As you hone these skills, you'll find that smart shopping not only lightens your financial load but also brings a sense of empowerment to the consumer experience.

# Chapter 8: Energy Efficiency at Home: Reduce Utility Bills

In a world where expenses seem to mount faster than we're able to contend with, managing and reducing utility bills can be both a relief and a necessity. By making your home more energy-efficient, you not only save money but also contribute positively to the environment.

This dual achievement is within your grasp with a few strategic adjustments. Let's explore some practical methods you can implement today to enhance energy efficiency and create a notable difference in your monthly outgoings.

Understanding Your Energy Usage

Interestingly enough, Before diving into solutions, it's essential to understand your current energy consumption. Start by examining your utility bills to identify patterns.

Are there particular months when your usage spikes? Consider investing in an energy monitor or utilizing energy assessment tools available through many utility providers. These tools can provide a detailed breakdown of your consumption, pinpointing which appliances or systems are the culprits of high energy usage.

Heating and Cooling Efficiency

Heating and cooling account for nearly half of the energy costs in an average home, making it a prime area for savings.

Here are some ways to make these systems more efficient:.

Many people don't realize this, but - **Programmable Thermostat**: Use a programmable thermostat to adjust the temperature automatically based on your schedule.

Set it to lower the heating or cooling when you're asleep or out of the house, and adjust to a comfortable level when you're home.

- **Seal and Insulate**: Drafts and poor insulation are leading reasons for energy loss. Check for air leaks around windows, doors, and in your attic.

Use weather stripping or caulk to seal these areas. Adding insulation, especially in the attic, can drastically improve your home's heat retention.

- **Ceiling Fans**: Utilize ceiling fans to circulate air.

In the summer, set them to rotate counterclockwise to create a cooling breeze, and reverse them in the winter to push warm air down.

Lighting and Electronics

Lighting and electronic devices make up a considerable portion of your electric bill. Small changes here can lead to significant savings:

- **LED Bulbs**: Swap out incandescent bulbs for LEDs.

LEDs use at least 75% less energy and last up to 25 times longer than traditional bulbs.

Interestingly enough, - **Smart Power Strips**: These can detect when devices are in standby mode and cut off power, reducing the phantom load, which is the energy electronics consume even when switched off.

- **Natural Light**: Make the most of natural light during the day.

Arrange workspaces and frequently occupied areas near windows. This not only reduces the need for artificial lighting but also improves your mood and productivity.

Water Heating Solutions

Let's not forget, Water heating is typically the second-largest energy expense in a home. Consider these adjustments:

- **Lower Water Heater Temperature**: Reduce your water heater's thermostat to 120 degrees Fahrenheit.

Each 10-degree reduction can save up to 5% on water heating costs.

- **Install Low-Flow Fixtures**: Low-flow showerheads and faucets can reduce water usage without sacrificing performance.

Look for the WaterSense label, which signifies both efficiency and performance.

- **Insulate Water Heater and Pipes**: Reduce heat loss by insulating your water heater, especially if it's an older model.

Insulating the first few feet of hot and cold water pipes can also save energy.

Appliances and Kitchens

The kitchen, being a hub of activity, can often be a significant energy user. Here are some tips to enhance efficiency:

- **Energy-Efficient Appliances**: When replacing appliances, choose those with the ENERGY STAR label, indicating they meet or exceed efficiency standards.

- **Optimal Use**: For dishwashers and washing machines, operate only with full loads to maximize the efficiency of each cycle.

Use cold water settings when possible, as most energy consumed by these machines is for heating water.

- **Microwaves Over Ovens**: Use a microwave or toaster oven for smaller meals; they use significantly less energy than a conventional oven.

Renewable Energy Options

If you're ready to make a long-term investment, consider renewable energy sources:

- **Solar Panels**: While the initial investment can be high, solar panels can drastically reduce your electricity bill and even allow you to sell excess power back to the grid in some areas.

It's worth noting that - **Solar Water Heaters**: These take advantage of the sun's rays to heat water, offering a significant savings on your energy bill.

Behavioral Changes and Maintenance

Sometimes, simple behavioral changes and regular maintenance can lead to impressive reductions in energy use:

Many people don't realize this, but - **Turn Off Unused Devices**: Get into the habit of turning off lights, appliances, and electronics when they're not in use.

Unplug chargers and other devices that continue to draw power.

- **Regular Maintenance**: Ensure that HVAC systems are serviced regularly, air filters are changed, and appliances operate efficiently.

- **Mindful Consumption**: Be mindful of energy use.

Simple actions like using a clothesline instead of a dryer and turning off lights when leaving a room can accumulate significant savings over time.

Conclusion

By implementing these energy-efficient practices, you're on your way to reducing your utility bills substantially. Every step you take contributes to a more sustainable future and a more manageable budget, ultimately fast-tracking you to financial stability and a robust emergency fund.

In the process, you'll find not only financial savings but also a refreshing sense of empowerment and responsibility towards the environment. Remember, energy efficiency isn't merely about cutting costs—it's about enhancing your lifestyle while making positive environmental choices.

# Chapter 9: Transportation Savings: Costs and Alternatives

Transportation is an essential component of modern life, offering the mobility and flexibility that facilitate our everyday activities.

However, it's also one of the key areas where many people can make significant savings. By examining transportation costs and exploring practical alternatives, you can effectively trim your expenses and bolster your emergency fund.

Understanding Transportation Costs

To begin, it's important to understand what constitutes transportation costs.

Ownership and operation of a vehicle includes not just the purchase price or monthly payments, but also insurance, fuel, maintenance, repairs, and even taxes and registration fees. For many, these represent a significant portion of monthly expenses.

Public transportation, while often more economical than owning a car, also comes with costs.

Monthly passes or individual trip fees can add up over time. Moreover, both car and public transportation users encounter indirect costs such as parking fees, tolls, and occasional rideshare expenses.

The first step towards savings is evaluating your transportation habits and expenses.

Review your bank statements or budget documents to catalog every transportation-related expense. Recognizing your patterns and how much you're spending is crucial for identifying areas where you can cut costs.

Reducing Vehicle Ownership Costs

For car owners, there are various ways to reduce transportation expenses without sacrificing convenience:

1. **Downsize Your Vehicle:** If possible, switch to a smaller, more fuel-efficient model.

The savings on fuel alone can be substantial. Consider a hybrid or electric vehicle if the cost is justified by lower fuel and maintenance costs.

As strange as it sounds, 2.

**Refinance or Pay Off Your Loan:** If you're making car payments, investigate whether refinancing for a lower rate is a viable option. Alternatively, focus on paying off your car loan to eliminate monthly payments sooner.

3. **Maintenance and Repair Costs:** Regular maintenance can prevent

costly repairs in the future.

Learn some basic car care like oil changes or tire rotations to save on labor costs. Compare prices and ask for recommendations when more significant repairs are necessary.

4. **Car Insurance Savings:** Shop around for car insurance.

Many providers offer discounts for safe drivers, bundling auto and home insurance, or even having certain safety features in your vehicle. Raising deductibles can also reduce premiums, but do this cautiously after weighing potential savings against out-of-pocket costs in the event of an accident.

Let's not forget, 5.

**Fuel Savings:** Keep your tires inflated and your engine tuned to improve fuel efficiency. Additionally, planning trips to avoid rush hours can save on gas and reduce unnecessary mileage.

Exploring Alternatives to Car Ownership

For those open to alternatives, exploring different modes of transportation can lead to substantial savings. Here are a few options:

Interestingly enough, 1. **Public Transportation:** If available in your area, public transport can be a more cost-effective and environmentally friendly alternative.

Monthly passes often offer discounts compared to daily tickets. Additionally, assess the feasibility of using public transit for part of your commute if a bus or train stop is near your workplace.

2.

**Carpooling:** Partnering with colleagues or neighbors for carpooling can directly cut your fuel and maintenance expenses. Carpool apps and platforms can help find others interested in sharing rides.

3. **Biking and Walking:** For shorter distances, consider biking or walking.

They are not only cost-effective but also excellent forms of exercise. Many cities now offer bike-sharing programs that make bicycles more accessible without ownership.

At first glance, 4.

**Ridesharing Services:** Services like Uber and Lyft can be a cheaper option on occasion compared to owning and maintaining a car, especially when combined with other transportation methods to reduce usage frequency.

5.

**Vehicle Sharing Services:** Companies like Zipcar provide vehicles for short-term use. This model is ideal for those who occasionally need a car, eliminating regular expenses like insurance and maintenance.

Navigating the Shift

Interestingly enough, Transitioning away from traditional car ownership or reducing transportation costs requires planning and often a change in habits.

Start by testing the waters—perhaps committing to using public transit one or two days a week before making a complete shift. Or, establish a carpool arrangement on a trial basis to see if it fits your routine.

Adjustments don't have to be immediate.

Small changes over time can lead to significant savings. Reevaluate these after a few months to gauge their impact on your finances and lifestyle.

Leveraging Technology

Let's not forget, Technology can be a vital ally in your quest for transportation savings. Numerous apps help track public transit schedules, find the cheapest gas, and offer carpool solutions.

Additionally, some apps analyze driving patterns to suggest efficiency improvements. Use these tools to maximize your efficiency and savings.

In summary, while transportation is necessary, its costs can be managed with careful planning and a willingness to explore alternatives.

Whether cutting down on vehicle ownership expenses or adopting new transportation methods, your efforts will not only trim your budget but also contribute significantly to building your emergency fund. The key is to make informed, strategic decisions that align with your lifestyle and goals.

# Chapter 10: Food and Dining: Eating Well on a Budget

Eating well on a budget is often seen as an elusive goal. With the rising costs of groceries and dining experiences, many people believe that cutting food expenses means compromising on quality or nutrition.

However, with some strategic planning and thoughtful choices, it's entirely possible to enjoy delicious meals without breaking the bank. This chapter will guide you through practical steps to trim your food expenses while still enjoying a varied and nutritious diet.

Understanding Your Food Expenses

At first glance, The first step in managing your food budget is understanding where your money is going. Break down your expenses into categories such as groceries, dining out, and food delivery services.

Look at your spending over the past few months to identify patterns and pinpoint areas where you can cut back. A clear picture of your current expenses will provide a baseline for setting realistic savings goals.

Meal Planning: The Cornerstone of Savings

Meal planning is one of the most effective strategies for reducing food costs. By dedicating some time each week to plan meals, you can avoid impulse buys and ensure that you only purchase what you will actually use.

Start with a simple list of recipes that you and your family enjoy. Consider themes for each night, such as Meatless Monday or Taco Tuesday, to simplify planning and make grocery shopping more efficient.

When planning your meals, focus on using seasonal produce and sales to guide your choices. Seasonal fruits and vegetables are often cheaper, tastier, and more nutritious than their off-season counterparts.

Check weekly grocery store flyers for sales and incorporate those deals into your meal plans. Over time, you'll become adept at adjusting your plans based on what's available and on sale.

Smart Grocery Shopping

Grocery shopping is where the bulk of your food budget is spent, so it pays to be strategic.

Start by creating a shopping list based on your meal plan, and stick to it. Impulse buys are one of the quickest ways to derail your budget.

It’s worth noting that Consider shopping at multiple stores to take advantage of the best deals. Discount grocery stores, farmer’s markets, and warehouse clubs can offer significant savings.

Be mindful of promotions, but be cautious of bulk buying unless you are certain you will use everything before it expires. It may also be beneficial to explore online grocery shopping for price comparison and convenience, but always be aware of delivery fees.

Coupons are an age-old tool for saving money, and digital coupons make it easier than ever to save without the hassle of clipping.

Many stores have apps or websites where you can load these coupons directly to your store loyalty card.

Cooking at Home: Economical and Enjoyable

Let's not forget, Cooking at home provides the greatest control over your food expenses.

Not only does it cost significantly less than eating out, but it also allows for healthier meal choices. Begin by mastering a few basic recipes that use inexpensive ingredients and can be easily adapted with what you have on hand.

Batch cooking is another useful strategy.

By preparing large quantities of a meal and storing portions for later, you save both time and money. Freezing individual portions of soups, stews, and casseroles can ensure that you always have affordable, home-cooked meals ready during busy times.

Learning to cook from scratch can also reduce costs.

Baking your own bread, making pasta sauce, or creating your own spice blends remove the premium you pay for pre-packaged versions. While this may take more time and effort, it can save a substantial amount over the long term.

Dining Out: Budget-Friendly Entertainment

Dining out is often viewed as a luxury, but with a few strategies, it can remain part of your lifestyle without derailing your savings goals.

First, consider limiting dining out to special occasions or setting a fixed monthly budget for this area. When you do dine out, take advantage of deals offered by restaurants, such as early bird specials or discounted days.

Consider opting for lunch instead of dinner when prices are typically lower, or skip the extras like drinks and dessert, which can quickly inflate the bill.

Also, look for restaurants that offer specials or loyalty programs that reward frequent customers with discounts or free meals.

As strange as it sounds, When making dining choices, prioritize quality over quantity.

Instead of dining out frequently, you might choose fewer outings but enjoy them at places that offer exceptional experiences or cuisine. This approach can make eating out feel more special and meaningful.

Keeping Track and Adjusting

As with any budget area, it's essential to track your food spending.

Utilize apps or spreadsheets to monitor your expenses and compare them against your budget targets. This tracking will highlight where you are succeeding and where you need to tighten further.

It's worth noting that Adjust your strategy as needed.

If you find that you consistently spend more in certain areas, revisit your meal planning or explore new ways to save. Flexibility and a willingness to adapt are crucial for sustained success in budget management.

Conclusion

Eating well on a budget is not only possible but can also lead to a healthier, more mindful way of living. With careful planning, shopping, and home cooking, you can enjoy flavorful and nutritious meals while steadily growing your savings.

Embrace the challenge as an opportunity to learn new skills and explore new culinary horizons. With time, you might find that not only can you save money, but you can also enrich your life through the joys of cooking and dining mindfully.

# Chapter 11: Managing Subscriptions and Memberships

In today's digital age, subscriptions and memberships have become a ubiquitous part of everyday life. From streaming services and gym memberships to magazine subscriptions and premium software, these recurring expenses can easily accumulate to a significant portion of your monthly outgoings.

While each subscription might seem affordable on its own, together they can silently erode your financial stability. Therefore, if you're intent on building your emergency fund quickly, a practical and effective strategy is to manage these subscriptions and memberships carefully. This chapter will guide you through assessing their value to you, identifying unnecessary expenses, and implementing strategies to reduce costs without sacrificing the quality of your lifestyle.

Conduct an Inventory

Interestingly enough, The first step towards managing subscriptions and memberships is to conduct a thorough inventory of everything you're subscribed to. This exercise might be revealing—you may discover subscriptions you had forgotten or no longer use.

Start by reviewing recent bank and credit card statements to identify any recurring charges. There are also several apps and digital tools available that can help automate this process, scanning your accounts for recurring transactions.

Once you've compiled a list, categorize each subscription.

This could include entertainment (such as Netflix or Spotify), fitness (such as gym memberships or yoga classes), lifestyle and services (such as meal kits or fashion boxes), and professional tools (such as software subscriptions or industry journals). Categorizing will help you better assess the value each subscription adds to your life and where you might most easily cut costs.

Evaluate Usage

Next, evaluate how often you actually use each of these subscriptions.

Be honest with yourself about your engagement and enjoyment, as it's easy to overestimate usage. Entertainment subscriptions are particularly susceptible to neglect; many people subscribe to multiple streaming services but only actively use one or two.

For gym memberships, consider if you're attending frequently enough to justify the cost.

If you visit only sporadically, it might be worth considering pay-per-use options or exploring free workout routines available online. For software or professional tools, determine whether you're leveraging all the features offered, or if a free or cheaper alternative might meet your needs.

Assess Value

Once you've determined your usage patterns, measure the value each subscription brings you.

This can be subjective but try to quantify it by asking yourself these questions: Does this subscription improve your quality of life? Does it contribute to your personal or professional goals? Would you truly miss it if you canceled or paused it?.

Subscriptions that align with your goals or significantly enrich your life should be prioritized.

On the other hand, those that you find yourself indifferent towards during this analysis might be prime candidates for removal. Be particularly wary of subscriptions that were impulse purchases or came with introductory offers that sounded too good to pass up but now don't provide significant value.

Consider Shared Accounts

A practical approach to reducing subscription costs without sacrificing access is to explore shared accounts. Many streaming services, for instance, permit multiple users or simultaneous streams on a single subscription.

If you have family or trustworthy friends with similar entertainment tastes, consider sharing the costs. Ensure that the subscription allows for this and that everyone involved agrees upfront to the arrangement to avoid potential complications.

For software subscriptions or professional tools, research multi-license options that might be cheaper per user if you and your colleagues or peers have similar needs.

Utilize Free Trials and Promotions

It's worth noting that Take advantage of free trials and promotional offers, but approach these with caution.

Set reminders to cancel before the trial ends to avoid unexpected charges if you find the service isn't worth it for you. Many companies offer substantial discounts or incentives to retain existing customers, so periodically check for any available promotions on subscriptions you value.

If negotiating periodically with customer service isn't appealing, sign up for email notifications from services to stay informed about deals.

Alternatively, consider canceling your subscription to see if a retention offer emerges. This strategy can sometimes secure lower rates or additional benefits.

Implement a Subscription Budget

Let's not forget, After evaluating and trimming your subscriptions, create a dedicated subscription budget within your overall monthly budget.

Allocating a specific amount for subscriptions will help prioritize spending according to value and usage, ensuring you maintain control over your monthly expenses. Review this budget periodically, at least bi-annually, to reflect any lifestyle changes or new services that enter or exit your life.

Practice Discipline

Discipline plays a crucial role in managing subscriptions effectively. Declutter regularly and resist the temptation to resubscribe without due diligence.

The convenience of having on-demand entertainment and services should not override financial sensibility. Keep impulse decisions in check by establishing a waiting period before signing up for a new subscription, allowing time to assess the necessity and value.

Conclusion

While subscriptions and memberships might seem like minor financial commitments individually, their cumulative impact can be significant. By conducting a thorough inventory, assessing usage and value, leveraging shared accounts, utilizing discounts, and budgeting wisely, you can gain control over these expenses.

Practicing discipline and making informed decisions about subscriptions can help redirect funds to your emergency savings, ensuring financial preparedness and security. Remember, the goal is not to strip away comforts and conveniences but to align them with conscious financial decisions that foster a resilient financial future. Through this focused approach, you'll be better equipped to boost your emergency fund effectively.

# Chapter 12: Nurturing Frugality: Hobbies and Entertainment

In our journey to fast-tracking savings and building an emergency fund, it's essential to consider how we can cultivate a satisfying life without sacrificing financial goals. Hobbies and entertainment are vital for personal growth and mental health, providing joy and a sense of accomplishment.

Yet, they are often seen as dispensable when cutting down expenses. In this chapter, we will explore how to embrace frugality while still enjoying meaningful leisure activities.

Redefining Pleasure

The perception that enjoyment equates to spending is deeply engrained in many of us. However, it's crucial to reassess what truly brings joy and satisfaction.

Take a moment to reflect on past experiences – often, the most fulfilling ones are not necessarily the most expensive. Drawing joy from simple, low-cost activities is the cornerstone of a frugal lifestyle.

For instance, reading is a rich and rewarding hobby that can come at little to no cost.

Libraries are a treasure trove of free resources, offering not just books but also e-books, audiobooks, movies, and even workshops. Getting a library card opens the door to a world of entertainment and learning opportunities without spending a dime.

Hobbies That Enrich and Save

In real life, One effective way to nurture frugality is to engage in hobbies that are not only low-cost but also provide value in terms of skills and self-sufficiency.

Cooking and gardening, for instance, are hobbies that can significantly reduce your monthly expenses. By growing your vegetables and cooking meals from scratch, you cultivate a healthier lifestyle while saving money on groceries.

Crafting is another hobby that exemplifies the blend of enjoyment and frugality.

Knitting, sewing, or woodworking can yield beautiful handmade items, often far superior in quality to mass-produced goods. Moreover, handmade gifts are more personal, eliminating the need to spend on expensive store-bought presents.

Leveraging Technology

In our digital age, technology can be a double-edged sword – a source of unnecessary expense or a tool for enriched, cost-effective living.

Streaming services and online platforms such as YouTube or Spotify can offer an affordable alternative to cable TV and high-cost entertainment. A carefully curated selection of entertainment subscriptions, aligned with your interests and strictly capped in terms of spending, can provide vast entertainment options for a fraction of the cost.

Moreover, numerous apps and websites offer free or low-cost courses on virtually any topic you're interested in, from learning a new language to coding or photography.

Dive into these resources to enhance your skills or discover new hobbies without the price tag of formal classes.

Socializing on a Budget

It's worth noting that Being frugal doesn't mean you have to cut social ties.

In fact, involving friends and family in your journey to cultivate low-cost hobbies can be a rewarding experience. Organizing a book club, hosting potluck dinners, or starting a community garden are excellent ways to remain socially active without spending lavishly.

Free community events, such as local festivals, museum nights, or public concerts, provide great opportunities to enjoy cultural enrichment and socialization.

Sign up for newsletters or follow community social media pages to stay informed about these happenings.

Minimalist Approach

Interestingly enough, Adopting a minimalist mindset can significantly impact both expenses and quality of life.

Focus on activities and items that offer maximum enjoyment and eliminate those that don't add value. For example, prioritize meaningful experiences like hiking a new trail or indulging in a captivating novel over impulse purchases or expensive outings that offer fleeting pleasure.

Create a 'gratitude journal' to regularly note activities that yield genuine joy.

Over time, this practice not only anchors you in positivity but also helps pinpoint which hobbies and entertainment choices truly enhance your life.

DIY Mindset

I've seen this happen before: Do-it-yourself is not merely a habit but a lifestyle that resonates with frugality.

Whether it's fixing minor repairs at home, creating art, or even refurbishing old furniture, a DIY mentality can cut costs and breed creativity. Countless online tutorials can guide you through projects, encouraging a hands-on approach to both leisure and everyday tasks.

This approach also extends to holiday celebrations and gifting. Handmade cookies or crafts embody personal thoughtfulness and sincerity, making special occasions enjoyable without excess expenditure.

Cultivating a Frugal Environment

It's worth noting that Surround yourself with individuals and communities that value frugality and simple living. These relationships can reinforce your goals, provide support, and inspire innovative ways to enjoy life without overspending.

Social media communities dedicated to frugal living offer daily tips and inspiration. Participate in these dialogues, share experiences, and learn from the journeys of like-minded individuals.

Moreover, living spaces influence entertainment habits; thus, creating an inviting, cozy home environment can minimize the desire to seek entertainment externally.

Declutter the space, introduce cozy lighting, and use multi-purpose furniture to enhance your home's functionality.

Conclusion

Nurturing frugality in hobbies and entertainment doesn't mean deprivation. It's about redefining pleasure, drawing fulfillment from simple joys, and living meaningfully within our means.

By embracing low-cost activities, socializing creatively, and harnessing technology wisely, we maintain balance and pave the way for financial security. Engaging with hobbies and entertainment frugally allows us to spend not only money but also time and energy wisely, ensuring we are investing in what truly enriches our lives.

In essence, nurturing frugality through hobbies and entertainment is a testament to resilience and creativity.

As you weave these practices into your routine, you set the foundation for a lifestyle that is both rewarding and financially prudent. Let this guide serve as a starting point to explore the myriad of low-cost possibilities and deepen your commitment to financial well-being.

# Chapter 13: Crushing Debt: Fast-Tracking Payments

If you're serious about boosting your emergency fund quickly, your journey must begin with a critical assessment of your current financial liabilities.

Debt can feel like a ball and chain attached to your finances, dragging down progress and stifling your ability to save effectively. This chapter will guide you through practical steps to crush your debt, enabling you to fast-track payments and liberate your financial resources to boost your emergency fund.

Understanding the Debt Landscape

Believe it or not, First, let's get an accurate picture of your debt landscape. Start by collating all your debts: credit cards, student loans, car loans, personal loans, and any other outstanding liabilities.

Create a debt inventory list that includes the creditor's name, total amount owed, interest rate, and minimum monthly payment for each debt. Understanding these details lays the foundation for a more informed and strategic debt repayment plan.

**Interest Rates Hold the Key**

Focus on the interest rates of your debts. High-interest debts, like those from credit cards, are financially hazardous and significantly complicate your ability to save.

When you recognize how interest accumulates, you'll understand why paying off high-interest debt should be a priority. The quicker you eliminate these debts, the less you'll pay in interest over time, freeing up funds for your emergency savings.

The Snowball and Avalanche Methods

With your debt inventory in hand, you have two primary methods for tackling debt, each with its unique strategies and psychological advantages: the Snowball Method and the Avalanche Method.

**The Snowball Method:** This method involves paying off your debts from the smallest balance to the largest. Start by making minimum payments on all debts except the one with the smallest balance.

Put any extra money towards eliminating this debt first. Once it's paid off, move on to the next smallest debt, snowballing the payment from the first debt into the next. The psychological benefit of experiencing quick wins can be incredibly motivating, encouraging you to persist.

Interestingly enough, **The Avalanche Method:** Conversely, the Avalanche Method prioritizes debts by interest rate, not balance. Focus on paying off the debt with the highest interest rate first while maintaining minimum payments on the rest.

Once the highest interest debt is paid, you transfer the payment towards the next highest interest debt. Although this method might not grant the immediate satisfaction of the Snowball Method, it does minimize interest payments and potentially save more money in the long run.

Both approaches are valid; the best choice depends on your financial situation and personal disposition.

Consider which method aligns better with your financial goals and emotional satisfaction.

Budgeting for Accelerated Debt Repayment

At first glance, For effective debt crushing, your budget needs to accommodate accelerated debt repayments.

Review your monthly expenses and identify where you can make temporary sacrifices to channel more money towards your debt. Look for areas to cut back: eating out less frequently, canceling subscription services, and curbing impulse purchases.

Create a realistic budget that ensures all minimum payments are met while allocating extra funds to your chosen priority debt.

Automating these payments can be beneficial, reducing the risk of missed payments and eliminating procrastination.

Side Hustles and Additional Income Streams

Sometimes, cutting expenses isn't enough, especially if you're dealing with significant debt. This is where side hustles or additional income streams become critical.

Consider offering freelance services in an area you excel, such as graphic design, writing, or consulting. Platforms like Upwork or Fiverr can connect you with clients actively seeking your services.

Alternatively, capitalize on the gig economy.

Drive for ride-sharing services, deliver groceries, or rent out a spare room through Airbnb. The additional income generated can accelerate your debt repayment strategy, contributing to faster financial freedom.

Negotiating with Creditors

Never underestimate the power of communication. Contact your creditors to negotiate better terms if you're struggling with high-interest rates or unaffordable minimum payments.

Credit card companies may be willing to lower interest rates or waive fees, especially if you have a history of timely payments. You can also discuss renegotiating loan terms, such as extended payment periods, to ensure the monthly payments fit more comfortably within your budget.

Credit counseling agencies can assist in this negotiation process, sometimes providing access to special debt management plans.

These agencies can advocate on your behalf to consolidate debts or secure reduced payment plans, alleviating immediate financial pressures.

Tracking Your Progress and Keeping the Momentum

To be honest, Tracking your progress is crucial for maintaining momentum on your journey to debt freedom. Regularly review your budget, debt balances, and progress towards your goals.

Witnessing tangible improvements can boost your motivation and help you stay committed to your strategy. Use apps or spreadsheets to monitor your debt payments and calculate the financial impact of your efforts.

Visualize your success by marking milestones on a chart or setting mini-goals along the way.

Celebrate these achievements with small, budget-friendly rewards that do not compromise your financial plans. Recognizing your dedication and sacrifice reinforces positive behaviors, encouraging you to maintain the path to debt freedom.

Preparing for Financial Challenges

I've seen this happen before: Understand that life is unpredictable. Even with the best-laid plans, unexpected financial challenges can arise, potentially derailing your efforts.

This is where your emergency fund plays a vital role. While you're fast-tracking your debt payments, it's critical to maintain a basic emergency savings threshold, a safety net against unforeseen expenses that could otherwise plunge you further into debt.

Aim to keep at least $1,000 in a readily accessible savings account until your high-interest debts are paid off.

Once those are settled, shift focus to grow your emergency fund further, ensuring you're better prepared for whatever life throws your way in the future.

Conclusion

Let's not forget, Crushing debt requires discipline, strategy, and perseverance. As you fast-track debt payments, you'll not only inch towards financial independence but also open up avenues to grow your emergency fund.

Embrace patience and resilience throughout this journey—each payment, sacrifice, and side hustle brings you closer to a financially secure future where debt no longer dictates your possibilities. Remember, the choices you make today will lay the groundwork for tomorrow's financial stability and peace of mind.

# Chapter 14: Building an Additional Income Stream

The journey towards financial security often requires creativity, persistence, and a willingness to step beyond your comfort zone.

In this chapter, we explore how establishing an additional income stream can expedite your saving goals and significantly bolster your emergency fund. While the task may sound daunting, we will break it into manageable sections and offer actionable insights to help you succeed.

Assess Your Skills and Interests

At first glance, The first step in building an additional income stream is a thorough self-assessment. Consider this your starting point.

Identify your skills, interests, and hobbies, and evaluate how they could translate into income-generating activities. Maybe you are a talented writer, have a knack for graphic design, or perhaps you're adept at crafts—anything that can provide a foundation for supplementary income.

Sit down with a pen and paper or open a digital document, and list everything you can think of. Don't censor yourself at this stage; even seemingly trivial skills or hobbies can prove valuable.

Once you've compiled a comprehensive list, prioritize them based on your proficiency and passion. This exercise is crucial because when you choose something you enjoy, it will be less of a chore and more of an enjoyable pursuit that brings in extra money.

Explore Freelancing and Remote Work Opportunities

I've seen this happen before: The digital age has made remote work and freelancing more accessible than ever.

Websites like Upwork, Fiverr, and Freelancer enable you to showcase your skills and attract clients from around the world. These platforms have a myriad of categories, ranging from writing and graphic design to programming and administrative assistance.

Set up a professional profile that highlights your expertise and past accomplishments. Adding work samples or a portfolio can significantly boost your visibility.

Start by bidding on smaller projects to build your reputation and gain positive reviews. As your profile grows, so will your opportunities for acquiring more lucrative jobs.

Remote work opportunities are also proliferating as companies increasingly adopt flexible working arrangements. Use job boards like Indeed, Remote.

co, or Glassdoor to find positions that align with your skills. Tailor your resume and cover letter for each application to improve your chances of landing a role.

Sell Products Online

Another excellent avenue of income generation is venturing into e-commerce.

If you have a product idea or can source products at a low cost, platforms like Etsy, eBay, Amazon, and Shopify allow you to reach a vast audience. This route requires upfront research and, occasionally, a small investment in inventory.

Start by identifying a niche market where you could potentially thrive. This might involve reviewing current trends, analyzing competitors, and determining the price points at which similar products are sold.

Once your research is complete, create or source your product and choose a suitable platform for your online store. Remember that branding and customer service can significantly influence your success, so invest time in creating a compelling online presence.

Offer Local Services

If you're more inclined towards offline work, consider offering services in your locality.

This could range from handyman work, dog walking, babysitting, or lawn care, to tutoring and teaching classes. A practical approach for these services is to leverage apps and online communities like TaskRabbit, Rover, or Nextdoor.

Advertise your services in local community centers, libraries, or on social media.

Word of mouth can be a potent tool—incentivize your existing clients to refer you to others by offering discounts or complimentary services.

Rent Out Assets

If you're looking for a more passive income stream, renting out your assets can be highly effective.

For instance, if you have extra space, platforms like Airbnb can help you rent a room or your entire home to travelers. Similarly, if you own high-end photography equipment, tools, or a vehicle that you don't frequently use, consider renting them out using platforms like Fat Llama or Turo.

Ensure you understand the local regulations and insurance implications before listing your items.

Protect your possessions with contracts and security deposits to prevent losses or damage.

Diversify Through Investments

While investment income might take longer to materialize, it's worth exploring.

By strategically investing in stocks, mutual funds, or real estate, you can create a long-term income stream. If this is new territory for you, consider consulting with a financial advisor to understand the risks and opportunities.

Starting with a small investment and gradually increasing your portfolio as you become more comfortable can help manage risk.

Apps like Acorns or Robinhood offer user-friendly platforms for beginner investors.

Balance and Time Management

As you embark on creating an additional income stream, maintaining a balance is crucial. If you're already employed full-time, you'll need to manage your new endeavor without compromising your primary job or personal life.

Outline a schedule to allocate time efficiently between these commitments. Remember that burnout is counterproductive; it's vital to maintain your health and well-being.

Using tools like Google Calendar, Trello, or Asana can assist in managing deadlines and tracking progress.

Delegate tasks when possible, and allow yourself breaks to prevent fatigue.

Setting Goals and Monitoring Progress

Define clear, measurable goals for your new income stream from the beginning.

Whether it's earning an extra $500 a month or contributing a specific amount to your emergency fund, setting these objectives provides motivation.

Track your progress regularly, noting what strategies work and where adjustments are necessary.

Monetary goals are tangible and allow you to celebrate achievements when you reach them, reinforcing your progress.

Conclusion

Building an additional income stream is a strategic move that can remarkably enhance your financial situation and expedite the growth of your emergency fund. It's about leveraging personal skills, capitalizing on modern technology and platforms, and persevering with discipline and commitment.

As you explore these avenues, stay patient, and remind yourself that you're not only increasing your income but also enriching your life with new experiences and skills. Your financial future may indeed rest not just on cutting expenses, but on the proactive development of new revenue streams.

# Chapter 15: Leveraging Technology for Financial Savings

In the digital age, technology isn't just a luxury; it's an essential tool in our daily lives, fundamentally transforming how we manage money.

Especially when you're looking to cut expenses and quickly boost your emergency fund, harnessing the power of technology can expedite the process. In this chapter, we explore how leveraging technology can help you achieve significant savings without compromising on your lifestyle's essential aspects.

**Smart Budgeting Apps**

It's worth noting that Gone are the days when budgeting involved elaborate spreadsheets and manual calculations. Today, numerous budgeting apps offer easy-to-use interfaces that help you monitor expenses and sustain a disciplined financial regimen.

Apps like Mint, YNAB (You Need a Budget), and EveryDollar allow you to track your income, categorize your expenses, and keep tabs on your savings objectives. They also offer notifications for bills due, help avoid late fees, and provide intelligent spending insights based on analyzed patterns. The beauty of these apps is their adaptability to your lifestyle, making budgeting less of a chore and more of an empowering habit.

**Automated Savings Tools**

Automation is a cornerstone of effective financial management. It's often easier to save when the process is out of sight, out of mind.

Tools like Acorns, Digit, and Chime automatically round up your purchases to the nearest dollar and save the difference. This "set it and forget it" concept can seamlessly accumulate substantial savings over time. Additionally, digital banks often offer features where you can set up automatic transfers from your checking to your savings account, effectively building your emergency fund without the need for active management.

**Price Comparison Websites and Extensions**

Before making any online purchase, take advantage of price comparison tools and browser extensions such as Honey, RetailMeNot, or InvisibleHand. These tools automatically scan for available coupons and monitor price variations across different platforms.

This simple addition to your digital shopping experience can result in significant cost-savings. Moreover, setting alerts for price drops on items you frequently purchase can ensure that you never pay more than necessary.

**Subscription and Recurring Expense Management**

As strange as it sounds, In the era of subscription services, it's easy to lose track of automatic payments draining your account.

Services such as Truebill and Trim assist in managing your subscriptions by identifying recurring charges—often those you've forgotten about—allowing you to cancel unwanted services. These apps can negotiate better rates for you, from lowering your utility bills to reducing the cost of your mobile plan, effectively trimming the fat of unnecessary expenses.

**Financial Education Platforms**

An often overlooked opportunity with technology is its educational potential. Platforms like Khan Academy, Coursera, and even YouTube host countless free courses and tutorials about financial literacy.

Whether it's learning how to invest wisely or understanding complex financial products, staying educated can prevent costly mistakes. It also empowers you with the knowledge to make smarter decisions about saving, spending, and safeguarding your wealth.

**Crypto and Investments Apps**

For those open to broader financial strategies, cryptocurrency and investment apps such as Coinbase, Robinhood, and E*TRADE provide opportunities to expand your portfolio with minimal initial investments.

These platforms make it possible to invest in fractional shares, lowering the barrier to entry for stock market participation. However, it's crucial to proceed with caution and ensure you fully understand the risks involved, aligning all investment decisions with your overall financial strategy.

**Telecommuting and Remote Work Opportunities**

I've seen this happen before: An indirect method of saving through technology is by exploiting telecommuting opportunities. Working from home decreases commute expenses, reduces the need for work attire, and allows for greater flexibility in balancing work-life commitments, affecting your food and childcare expenses positively.

With thousands of remote job portals and communities, such as Remote. co and FlexJobs, finding a suitable telecommuting role is more accessible than ever.

**Telehealth Services**

Healthcare is a significant expense for many, but technology offers an alternative through telehealth services.

Platforms like Teladoc and Amwell provide affordable, convenient access to medical professionals without the need for in-person visits. By using technology to manage health expenses, you can potentially reduce unnecessary spending, allocate more to your savings fund, and still prioritize your well-being.

**Gamifying Savings with Apps**

Some people might find traditional saving methods monotonous and unengaging.

Apps like Qapital and Long Game apply gamification principles to saving money, helping to turn saving into a rewarding challenge rather than a tedious task. These apps employ triggers, goals, and even games where depositing more money potentially enhances the user experience, thereby encouraging a stronger commitment to saving.

**Energy and Household Management Tools**

Many people don't realize this, but Smart home technologies like programmable thermostats, energy-efficient appliances, and intelligent lighting systems drastically cut down on energy expenditures.

Appliances that connect to your phone offer fine-grained control over energy use, ensuring you only consume what's necessary. These smart systems might require a preliminary setup investment but often lead to long-term savings, ultimately creating more room in your budget for saving.

**Ride-hailing and Car-sharing Apps**

Transportation costs are another significant lump in budgets.

With apps like Uber, Lyft, and Zipcar, it's possible to efficiently manage transportation expenses through ride-hailing or car-sharing options. Instead of dealing with the costs of owership—insurance, maintenance, and fuel—you could resort to these services when commuting, drastically transforming discretionary spending.

**Conclusion: Integrating Tech into Your Financial Plan**

Effectively utilizing technology for savings requires more than just downloading apps; it demands integration into your financial routines. As you harness these digital tools, maintain mindfulness regarding data privacy and security.

Regularly review settings, use strong, unique passwords, and when possible, activate two-factor authentication to protect your financial information. A strategic blend of well-chosen technology solutions can guide you toward swiftly increasing your emergency fund without curtailing quality of life. In the digital era, technology can make the path to financial health accessible, efficient, and sustainable.

# Chapter 16: Investing in Yourself: Skills to Save More

In the journey to build a robust emergency fund, cutting expenses and saving more are crucial steps. However, there's another powerful yet often overlooked strategy: investing in yourself.

Enhancing your skills doesn't just lead to personal growth and professional advancement; it can also lead to significant cost savings. By becoming more skillful and resourceful, you can reduce dependency on external services, make more informed financial decisions, and even create additional income streams. This chapter will explore practical skills you can develop to improve your financial well-being.

1. Mastering Financial Literacy

Financial literacy is foundational for anyone looking to enhance their savings and manage their finances effectively. Understanding the principles of budgeting, saving, investing, and debt management empowers you to make informed decisions about your money.

To improve your financial literacy, consider taking courses, reading books, or listening to podcasts on personal finance. Websites like Coursera, Udemy, or even local community colleges often offer inexpensive or even free courses. Becoming financially literate not only helps prevent common financial mistakes but also enables you to spot opportunities to save and invest wisely.

2. Learning DIY Skills

Home repairs, car maintenance, or even basic sewing are skills that can lead to substantial savings. Hiring professionals for every minor repair or alteration can quickly add up. By learning to fix leaky faucets, change your car's oil, or sew a button, you can save hundreds of dollars annually.

Online platforms like YouTube offer free tutorials for virtually any DIY project you can think of. Start small and gradually build your confidence to tackle bigger projects. Not only will you save money, but you'll also gain a sense of satisfaction and independence.

3. Cooking and Meal Planning

Food is a significant expense for most households, and dining out or ordering in can quickly deplete your savings. Learning to cook at home and effectively plan meals can greatly reduce your grocery bills. Begin with simple recipes and gradually expand your repertoire.

Meal planning can minimize food waste and help you make more intentional grocery purchases, thus avoiding impulsive or unnecessary buy. Websites like AllRecipes or Budget Bytes offer cost-effective meal ideas with clear step-by-step instructions. Additionally, cooking at home is generally healthier, which could also lead to savings on healthcare over time.

4. Negotiation Skills

Whether it's your salary, a car purchase, or your cable bill, being able to negotiate effectively can have a direct impact on your finances. Many people are uncomfortable with negotiation, yet it's a skill that can be learned and perfected with practice.

Start small by negotiating bills or service contracts and gradually build up to bigger financial transactions. There are numerous resources available, including books like "Getting to Yes" by Roger Fisher and William Ury, which provide strategies to help you negotiate better terms in various aspects of life.

5. Tech-Savviness

In today's digital economy, being tech-savvy can significantly cut costs and boost efficiency. Learn to use budgeting apps like Mint or YNAB (You Need a Budget) to track expenses and set saving goals.

Familiarity with technology also allows you to take advantage of apps and websites that offer discounts, cashback, or price comparisons. Moreover, developing tech skills can enhance your professional qualifications, potentially leading to better-paying job opportunities. Start by focusing on essential skills like using office software, understanding cloud storage, or learning basic coding through platforms like Codecademy or Khan Academy.

6. Time Management

Time is one of your most valuable resources. Learning to manage it effectively can lead to more productive days and less stress, allowing you to focus on both earning and saving more.

Time management skills can reduce procrastination and increase productivity at work, potentially leading to salary increases or business growth. Tools like Google Calendar, Trello, or the Pomodoro Technique can help you optimize daily schedules and deadlines, ensuring efficient use of time to enhance your financial endeavors.

7. Networking and Communication

Let's not forget, Building strong communication skills and networking proficiency doesn't only open doors to new career opportunities; it also puts you in touch with new ideas, perspectives, and advice. By expanding your network, you might gain access to side gigs or freelancing opportunities that supplement your income.

Attend industry events, join professional groups, or engage in social media platforms related to your field of interest. Good communication skills can also enhance your negotiation abilities, help you articulate your ideas more clearly, and build professional relationships that could provide financial insights and opportunities.

8. Gardening and Sustainability Practices

Sustainability isn't just beneficial for the environment; it can be cost-effective too. If you have space, starting a small garden can provide fresh produce, reducing your grocery bills.

Even without a yard, balcony or window gardens for herbs and small vegetables can be very economical. Exploring practices such as composting, rainwater collection, or energy conservation can reduce utility expenses. Numerous community classes or online resources like The Spruce offer guidance on starting sustainable practices without a significant initial investment.

Final Thoughts

Investing in yourself is an ongoing journey with compounding benefits. The skills you choose to develop will not only help you save money but can also enrich your life, providing both personal satisfaction and professional growth.

Educate yourself, embrace a DIY mentality, and leverage technology to stay ahead. By continuously investing in your skills, you cultivate a versatile toolkit that empowers you to manage finances more effectively, thus fast-tracking your path to a substantial emergency fund. Remember, the greatest investment you can make is in yourself—it pays the best interest.

# Chapter 17: Banking Smarter: Maximizing Account Benefits

In today's fast-paced and financially unpredictable world, making the most out of your banking options can be a game changer for building an emergency fund swiftly. Banks are not just places to deposit your income; they can be a launchpad for financial efficiency and savings.

To tap into this potential, you need to think beyond the mundane view of a checking account as a mere storage facility. Instead, explore the options that maximize benefits and work diligently to optimize every single aspect of your banking experience.

To begin with, selecting the right type of account is paramount. Traditional savings and checking accounts are ubiquitous, but there is a broad spectrum of specialized accounts offering various advantages.

High-yield savings accounts, for example, provide higher interest rates than standard savings accounts, allowing your money to grow faster with minimal effort on your part. Credit unions often present another attractive alternative, typically offering lower fees and better rates because they are member-owned, focusing on serving their members rather than making a profit.

Many people don't realize this, but But choosing the right account is just the start. Once you've zeroed in on the account type that suits your needs, pay attention to the details in your bank's fine print. The services that banks bundle with their accounts can significantly impact your financial health.

These services might include overdraft protection, which shields you from hefty fees if you accidentally spend a bit more than what's in your account. While often automatic, it's critical to understand its cost implications. Some banks charge per occurrence, while others offer it as a complimentary service linked to a savings account.

Additionally, embracing technology through mobile banking apps can dramatically reshape the way you manage your accounts. Most banks offer free apps that allow for real-time tracking of expenses, remote check deposits, bill payments, and budgeting tools.

By regularly monitoring your accounts, you gain invaluable insight into your spending habits, which is a crucial step toward adjusting and optimizing your finances for faster savings accumulation. Take the time every week to review your bank statements and understand where your money is going. This routine can help you catch errors or fraudulent activity, and avoid unnecessary fees.

Loyalty can also play a powerful role in maximizing account benefits. Some banks reward long-term account holders with advantages such as better interest rates, waived fees, or access to premium account features.

If your bank offers a loyalty program or tiers of membership, inquire how you can make the most of it. Often, these benefits are not heavily advertised, so professing interest can sometimes unlock otherwise dormant possibilities.

As strange as it sounds, Let's not forget the allure of cashback and rewards programs. Increasingly, banks are pairing their debit and checking accounts with incentives that reward users for their spending patterns.

By selecting accounts that correlate well with your regular expenses, like groceries or gas, you can capitalize on these benefits. However, always weigh these rewards against any potential fees or conditions that might erode their value.

Furthermore, consolidating your financial life by opting for a single bank can result in assorted advantages. Many banks offer deals for customers who open multiple account types with them, such as checking, savings, and credit card accounts.

By consolidating, you might enjoy reduced banking fees, more favorable interest rates, and streamlined management of your financial portfolio. That being said, ensure that the combined benefits outweigh the often higher fees that can come from having multiple products with one provider.

One often overlooked feature is automatic transfers. Set up regular, automatic transfers from your checking to your savings account.

This setup ensures that you are saving consistently without having to consciously decide to do so each time. Even small amounts, transferred routinely, can accumulate quickly, aiding in the quick establishment of a robust emergency fund.

Many people don’t realize this, but Lastly, one should always be on the lookout for emerging banking innovations. The financial technology (fintech) revolution has injected fierce competition into the banking industry, driving down fees and spurring the creation of products tailored to the needs of the modern consumer.

Neobanks, or digital-only banks, often feature user-friendly apps with advanced functionalities such as AI-driven savings plans and personalized financial advice. They typically have lower overhead costs and pass these savings on to consumers in the form of lower fees and higher rates.

Understanding and maximizing the benefits of your bank accounts requires a proactive and informed approach. By conducting a thorough analysis of your current accounts, exploring new offerings, and utilizing the digital tools at your disposal, you can significantly enhance the management of your finances.

Banking smarter is not just about where you save; it is about leveraging the full suite of features and understanding the subtle interplay of fees, interest, and perks to build your emergency fund with speed and efficacy. The banks are there to serve you—ensure that this service is as advantageous and profitable as possible to your savings quest.

# Chapter 18: Saving on Insurance: Reevaluating Coverage

In our quest to build a robust emergency fund, reassessing every nook and cranny of our financial existence is crucial. One often overlooked aspect is insurance.

While necessary for safeguarding against unforeseen events, insurance premiums can weigh heavily on your monthly budget. However, with careful reevaluation of coverage, significant savings can be realized.

Understand What You Have

To be honest, Before diving into changes, equip yourself with knowledge.

Begin by gathering all current insurance policies—auto, home, renters, health, life, and any others pertinent to your situation. Breakdown each policy, paying attention to the type of coverage, premium amounts, deductibles, and additional riders or features.

Evaluate Actual Needs

With your policies laid out, meticulously assess your needs based on your current lifestyle and financial circumstances.

Insurance needs evolve, meaning coverage purchased a decade ago may no longer align with your requirements. Here are some considerations:.

It's worth noting that - **Homeowners/Renters Insurance:** Evaluate the value of your possessions and the changing risk levels associated with your location.

Have you acquired valuable assets, or have any employees or residents changed? Security upgrades at home, like alarm systems and safety locks, can sometimes lower premiums.

- **Auto Insurance:** Compare your car's current market value against the coverage cost.

If your car is older, comprehensive or collision coverage may not be necessary. Also consider your driving habits; if you've moved to a less traffic-heavy area or drive fewer miles, you might qualify for lower rates.

- **Health Insurance:** Analyze your health needs.

Are there chronic conditions that necessitate higher coverage, or are you young and healthy, preferring to opt for a high-deductible plan paired with a Health Savings Account (HSA)?.

Interestingly enough, - **Life Insurance:** The purpose here is to secure your dependents' future or to cover debts.

If your children have grown and become independent, or if you've paid off significant debts, your life insurance needs may decrease.

Shop Around

Insurance is a competitive market; providers are constantly adjusting rates to attract or retain customers. This is your opportunity to shop around.

Comparing quotes from different companies can reveal cost disparities. Make use of online comparison tools to easily scout for potential savings, but be sure to evaluate the coverage terms—cheaper isn't better if it's inadequate for your needs.

Bundle Where Possible

Many insurers offer substantial discounts when you bundle multiple policies together.

You may have separate providers for your home and auto insurance, but chances are, consolidating these under one provider can lead to discounts. It's a cost-effective strategy that doesn't compromise your coverage needs.

Raise Deductibles

Many people don't realize this, but If you maintain a healthy emergency fund, consider raising your deductibles. This will immediately decrease your premiums.

Ensure your emergency fund can absorb these higher deductibles when the need arises. This balance is essential—don't raise them beyond what you could manage comfortably in an emergency.

Review Annually

Insurance needs are not static.

Making it a point to annually review and reassess your insurance can yield continued savings. Life changes, market trends, and new product offerings can all impact your needs and eligibility, transforming your insurance portfolio into a more cost-effective and appropriately tailored set of protections.

Utilize Discounts

Many insurers offer numerous discounts based on various personal circumstances and preventative actions.

Installing smoke detectors, burglar alarms, or taking defensive driving courses are small investments that can lead to significant savings on premiums. Similarly, many employers or organizations have partnerships that include insurance discounts—always inquire about workplace or membership perks.

Consider Liability Limitations

In real life, In the pursuit of economizing on insurance, it's crucial to not skimp on liability coverage, particularly for home and auto insurance.

Lawsuits can drastically deplete your financial resources if your coverage is insufficient. Ensure you carry enough liability protection to comfortably cover at least the value of your total assets.

Keep an Eye on Credit

Insurers often use credit scores as a factor in determining premiums.

By maintaining good credit, you make yourself eligible for better rates. Regularly check your credit report for errors and continue to manage debt wisely.

Engaging with a Broker

An insurance broker can be an ally in dissecting the maze of insurance.

They have access to numerous insurance products and can help align policies with your financial goals. While they may charge a fee, the long-term savings and peace of mind offered can often outweigh the cost.

Limit Underinsurance Risk

To be honest, It's possible to cut premiums by minimizing coverage, but guard against underinsurance.

Having a policy that doesn't fully cover your needs in a crisis can be financially ruinous.

Conclusion

By taking a proactive stance on managing insurance, you can significantly reduce your monthly expenses thereby funneling additional resources into your emergency fund. Remember, the essence of insurance lies in protection; with deliberate methods, it can be cost-efficient without sacrificing your security net.

Reevaluate your coverage today to ensure you're not overpaying tomorrow. Save smartly, protect prudently, and watch as your financial resilience strengthens.

# Chapter 19: Establishing and Growing Your Emergency Fund

When life throws a curveball, an emergency fund can be your financial safety net, transforming potential crises into manageable inconveniences. Having an emergency fund is not just a cornerstone of sound financial planning; it is a necessity that grants peace of mind and security.

If you're reading this chapter, you've likely decided it's time to establish or bulk up your emergency fund. This decision is pivotal, and this chapter will guide you through practical steps to make it happen efficiently and effectively.

The Basics: Understanding the Emergency Fund

I've seen this happen before: An emergency fund is a savings account earmarked for unplanned expenses, which could range from medical emergencies to sudden car repairs or unexpected job loss. Why keep it separate from your regular savings? Simplicity.

By having a clearly defined account for emergencies, you reduce the temptation to dip into these funds for non-essentials. Aim to save an amount that would cover three to six months' worth of living expenses. However, starting with a smaller goal, such as $1000, is perfectly acceptable and serves as a reasonable initial buffer.

Step-by-Step Guide to Establishing an Emergency Fund

1. **Assess Your Monthly Expenses**: The first step is to calculate your average monthly expenses.

Be thorough—include rent or mortgage, utilities, groceries, insurance, transportation, debt repayments, and any other regularly occurring costs. This will help you determine your ultimate emergency fund goal.

I've seen this happen before: 2. **Set a Realistic Starting Goal**: For many, the figure of three to six months of expenses can initially seem daunting.

An attainable target, like $1,000, can provide motivation and a sense of accomplishment upon completion. Once reached, consider increasing your goal incrementally.

3. **Open a Dedicated Savings Account**: Designate a separate high-yield savings account specifically for your emergency funds.

Online banks often offer higher interest rates compared to traditional banks, helping your money grow over time. Ensure the account allows for easy access but doesn't encourage impulsive withdrawals.

4. **Automate Savings**: Automation simplifies the savings process and ensures consistency.

Set up automatic transfers from your checking to your dedicated savings account on payday. Direct depositing even a small, consistent amount can significantly impact over time.

I've seen this happen before: 5.

**Track Spending and Cut Costs**: Review your expenses to identify areas where you can cut back, funneling those savings into your emergency fund. Tools like budgeting apps can help you track and categorize spending, making it easier to spot areas ripe for trimming.

6.

**Increase Income Sources**: Consider avenues to boost your income—whether through part-time work, freelance projects, or monetizing hobbies. Dedicate extra earnings directly to your emergency fund to accelerate its growth.

Growing Your Emergency Fund

Let's not forget, Once you've established an emergency fund, the next challenge is to grow it to a sustainable size—ideally one that can fully cover three to six months' worth of expenses.

Here are some strategies to consider:.

1.

**Reevaluate and Adjust Goals Regularly**: Financial situations and expenses evolve. Periodically reassess your fund goal to ensure it aligns with current living costs and lifestyle changes.

2.

**Windfalls and Bonuses**: Tax refunds, work bonuses, or any financial windfall should be directed, fully or partially, toward your emergency fund. While it may be tempting to splurge, consider your fund a priority investment in your stability.

In real life, 3.

**Side Hustle Earnings**: Leverage the gig economy to your advantage. Part-time work or freelance projects can generate significant supplemental income dedicated explicitly to fortifying your emergency fund.

4.

**Lifestyle Adjustments**: Small, sustainable changes can accumulate significant savings. Substituting homemade coffee for daily café visits or utilizing public transport might seem minor, but these adjustments meaningfully contribute over time.

5. **Regular Contributions**: Even as little as $10 a week adds up over a year.

Maintain a standing order in your budget to add what you can regularly. The discipline of regular contributions lays a strong foundation for financial security.

In real life, 6.

**Review and Celebrate Milestones**: Every milestone hit is an affirmation of your discipline and effort. Celebrate these successes—it reaffirms the value of your hard work and keeps your motivation high.

Leveraging Your Fund: When to Use It

Understanding when to utilize your emergency fund is just as crucial as establishing it.

Emergencies are significant, unforeseen costs—not predictable expenses like routine maintenance or anticipated job changes. Always consider the potential for replenishment after use; this fund's purpose is to bridge finite challenges, not habitual or minor disruptions in cash flow.

Conclusion: A Shield Against the Unpredictable

Building an emergency fund won't happen overnight. It requires patience, discipline, and occasionally sacrificing immediate comforts for longer-term security.

The benefits, however, are unequivocal. More than financial backing, a robust emergency fund offers personal peace, equipping you to handle life's unpredictability with confidence and composure.

As you walk through these steps, remember this fund is a testament to your foresight and resilience.

It is an assurance of stability in an unpredictable world—a judicious measure that turns the unknown from a looming anxiety into a manageable certainty. Make this commitment now, and future you will thank you.

# Chapter 20: Maintaining Momentum: Long-Term Financial Health

Maintaining momentum in personal finance is akin to keeping the wheels of a well-oiled machine turning smoothly.

You've laid down the groundwork, established routines, and perhaps even seen the gratifying first results of your efforts. But how do you ensure that the progress you've made doesn't stall and that your financial health continues to thrive over the long term? This chapter is dedicated to providing practical strategies for sustaining the momentum you've built and fostering lasting financial well-being.

Understanding the Importance of Momentum

Believe it or not, Before delving into specific strategies, it's crucial to acknowledge why maintaining momentum is essential. Just as in exercise or education, consistency in financial habits leads to compound results over time.

The same $50 you save today grows into more significant savings and investment returns tomorrow. The discipline you exercise in managing your finances not only creates security but also propels you toward greater financial goals.

Establishing Clear, Evolving Goals

The first step in sustaining momentum is to periodically revisit and update your financial goals. What was urgent or important a year ago may no longer hold the same significance today.

To ensure you're always working toward something meaningful, set aside time every six months or annually to review and adjust your financial goals. This practice will ensure your efforts remain relevant and motivate you to continue pushing forward.

Believe it or not, Start by re-evaluating your short-term, medium-term, and long-term goals. Have you achieved any? Do others need adjustment? Perhaps you initially aimed to build a $1,000 emergency fund.

Upon reaching that milestone, consider expanding the goal to six months' worth of living expenses. By updating your objectives, you maintain a sense of purpose and direction.

Creating a Sustainable Budget Framework

After redefining your goals, it's essential to adapt your budgeting strategy to match your evolving financial landscape.

A rigid budget might stifle your progress instead of promoting it. Consider establishing a flexible budgeting framework that allows you to adapt to changes in income, expenses, and priorities without veering off course.

Divide your budget into fixed and variable expenses, allowing room for adjustments. A flexible framework caters to changing needs and ensures continued adherence to your financial plan.

Utilize tools such as budgeting apps and expense trackers to keep a real-time pulse on your finances. These tools provide insights into spending habits, reveal potential areas for improvement, and prevent unnecessary splurges.

Automating Savings and Investments

One of the most effective ways to maintain momentum is through automation. Automating savings and investment contributions ensures consistency and reduces the temptation to spend what should be saved.

Set up automatic transfers to your savings account or retirement fund on the same day you receive your salary. By treating savings as a non-negotiable "expense," you're guaranteeing regular contributions toward your future.

Don't stop at savings; consider automating bill payments and other regular financial tasks.

This automation minimizes risks associated with late fees, enhances your credit score, and frees up mental energy to focus on more strategic financial planning.

Leveraging Financial Tools and Resources

Technology offers a plethora of tools designed to enhance financial management and decision-making.

From expense-tracking applications to robo-advisor investment platforms, leveraging these resources can simplify your financial life and maintain your momentum.

I've seen this happen before: Explore financial dashboards that consolidate your financial accounts, providing comprehensive visibility into your net worth, expenditure, and investment performance.

By having a panoramic view of your finances, you can make informed decisions conducive to long-term health.

Building a Strong Financial Network

Maintaining momentum is not an isolated endeavor; building a financial support network adds accountability and motivation.

Share your financial goals and milestones with trusted friends or family members who can provide encouragement and objective advice.

Consider joining personal finance forums or communities where like-minded individuals discuss strategies, challenges, and successes.

These platforms facilitate the exchange of experiences and solutions, enabling you to learn from others while sharing your journey.

Encouraging Lifelong Financial Learning

Continuing education plays a pivotal role in sustaining financial momentum.

Dedicate time to improve your financial literacy by consuming reputable books, podcasts, and articles on personal finance topics. Understanding subjects like investing, tax strategies, and retirement planning equips you with the knowledge to make sound decisions and adapt to changing financial landscapes.

As strange as it sounds, Educational workshops or webinars also serve as valuable resources for improving financial competencies.

Attend events that cover the latest economic trends or investment opportunities to stay informed and make proactive adjustments to your financial plan.

Celebrating Milestones and Progress

Finally, celebrate the milestones you achieve along your financial journey.

While it's easy to get lost in the pursuit of long-term objectives, acknowledging small achievements reinforces positive financial habits and fuels further progress.

To be honest, Consider adopting a reward system where reaching a specific goal allows for a modest, planned indulgence.

Whether it's a small vacation or dining at your favorite restaurant, celebrating milestones keeps you motivated and passionate about your financial journey.

Staying Adaptable and Resilient

In the realm of personal finance, the only constant is change.

Economic conditions fluctuate, unexpected expenses arise, and life circumstances evolve. Maintaining momentum necessitates resilience and adaptability to navigate these changes effectively.

Cultivate a mindset that embraces change as an opportunity for growth rather than an insurmountable obstacle.

Develop contingency plans to address potential setbacks without veering off course from your financial objectives. By remaining flexible and proactive, you'll be better equipped to sustain momentum and achieve lasting financial health.

Conclusion

Sustaining the momentum you've built is no small feat, but with clear goals, automated systems, continual learning, and a supportive network, it is entirely achievable.

By implementing these strategies, you not only ensure long-term financial health but also pave the way for achieving greater financial independence and peace of mind. As you continue your journey, remember that the habits and mindset you cultivate today lay the foundation for a prosperous tomorrow.

# About the Author

T. S. AVINI is a writer who believes in the power of sharing life's lessons. Having faced hardship and pain, he turned to writing as a form of self-expression and healing. Today, he pours his heart into every book, aiming to help others navigate their own struggles and find strength in vulnerability.

www.ingramcontent.com/pod-product-compliance
Lightning Source LLC
LaVergne TN
LVHW050748061126
851857LV00013B/1049
*9791257828080*